Paradisal Plums
Peaceful Ponderings from a (Rebel) Pandit's Puce Palm
[Aphorisms, Adages, and Analects of Sri Adi Dadi]

Volume I

compiled and edited by
Etbonan Karta

Copyright © 2001 revised and updated edition **Orange Palm Publications**
First edition 1995 by the Poorna Jnana Yoga Foundation Inc.©
        under Original Title: *Paradisal Plums to Ponder Upon and Eat*

All rights reserved. No part of this book may be reproduced in any form without permission in writing from the author, except to quote or photocopy specific passages for the purposes of group study.

Orange Palm and Magnificent Magus Publications Inc.©

Mailing address: Canadian Ashram of Occult and Spiritual Sciences©
5825 Sherbrooke East, Unit 7, Montreal, Quebec, H1N 1B3
Telephone: (514) 255-0109
Facsimile: (514) 255-0478
Web site: http://www.fondationpjy.ca

Paradisal Plums
Peaceful Ponderings from a (Rebel) Pandit's Puce Palm
Volume ISBN: 0-9687048-1-6
Collection ISBN: 0-9687048-3-2

Printed in Canada
Printed and bound March 2001 by *AGMV Marquis, membre du Groupe Scabrini.*

Dedicated to the S<small>ELF</small>, the Guru, in every man

Special Thanks:

Thanks to lilting Lou for the book layout, typing, typing and re-typing, and for her impeccable patience and utmost perseverance; thanks also to Joyful Jyoti Joss and Light-Bulb Luce for the lovely book cover and the plum bushels, branches and blooms that delicately illustrate the pages.

Forthcoming books by **Magnificent Magus Publications:**

Scriptings of the Soul in Questions of Light by Dadi Darshan Dharma

The Divine Concordance of Light: A Handbook from Heaven to Progression Earth by Etbonan Karta

The Science of Invocation and the Art of Affirmation, invocatory prayers by Sri Adi Dadi, compiled by Etbonan Karta. (To be used as a companion book to *The Divine Concordance of Light*)

Forthcoming books by **Orange Palm Publications:**

Original-Face, Contemporary Koans from the Boffola Belly of Pu'Tai by Sri Adi Dadi

Paradoxes of D.D.D. by Sri Adi Dadi

Paradisal Plums: Peaceful Ponderings from a (Rebel) Pandit's Puce Palm, Volumes 3, 4, Aphorisms, Adages, and Analects of Sri Adi Dadi (also compiled and edited by Etbonan Karta)

Foreword

Sri Adi Dadi's genius is genuine.

The hidden, often humorous *original face* of the genie within him twinkles like a star in the smiling skies of his very blue eyes.

His physicality is quite ordinary, his way is rather unassuming, his presence, quietly disquieting.

He is known to be a living Wisdom Teacher of rare caliber, always full of Divine sparklings, and is said to be giving out the very ancient Truth, in an East-meets-West modern tonality, and with an authentic resonance of the Real.

He claims however, to still be working diligently on the ongoing practice of always-already being Compassionate at all times, and in all circumstances.

Sri Adi Dadi wrote the whole of his 3,000 entries of "Paradisal Plums" within a brief period spanning about 4½ months... that is to say, between mid-December '91 to the end of April '92... whilst keeping an extremely active schedule of speaking engagements and weekend seminars.

Ideas would flow down at times so rapidly and spontaneously, that within a brief 2-3 hour period, some 68 'Plums' of all shapes and sizes would plummet down into the receptive basket of his creative Consciousness... and all too soon, sometimes within a week, a whole 'Bushel' would be filled.

The reader's regular perusal, and intelligent contemplation of the spiritual 'Plums' that are strewn about in the book, in an always spontaneous, but orderly fashion, promises to help the spiritualizing process in all serious students of esoteric lore, as well as all seekers of God, to become ever more firmly rooted (mind & heart) in the Divine.

From a level-headed, high level of Consciousness, Sri Adi Dadi once wrote:

"The Glory of the Cross is my decreed death; the Folly of the Cross is my (already) forgotten life."

This Divinely *enigmatic man*, called Master by some, and known at times as D.D.D., seems to have a spiritually sobering and charismatic effect upon all who are fortunate enough to cross his Path.

May the reader presently enjoy these first two modest volumes of Sri Adi Dadi, the Rebel Pandit's, "Paradisal Plums".

PARADISAL PLUMS

FIRST BUSHEL

DECEMBER 4 - 13, 1991

I
Know Less
Comprehend More

The Seeker needs to know less, and to comprehend more of the little he (thinks) he knows.

2
Ocean of Life

In order for the Seeker to go from the shore of concrete limitedness to the great shore of Immortal Beingness, the wave-like, and often storm-tossed ocean of Life must be accommodated, traversed, befriended, understood and loved... and in the final few, exhaustive miles of incarnated existence, ineluctably Mastered.

3
(Both) a Comfort and Distraction

Knowledge becomes (both) a comfort and a distraction, once you cozy up to its fire, and stay overnight.

4
Twin Peaks

The capacity to Understand is firmly planted upon the twin peaks of knowledge and experience.

5
The Good True and Beautiful

All that is good and true and beautiful is Innocently unselfconscious.

6
The Excusing Self

The starting sadhak often has the bad habit of exempting and excusing his own self from the pointing finger of life's stories, as spoken about by the Teacher.

7
Magical Time

A magical time does come in satsang, when the Teacher is able to employ the creative tension of Silence… between words, between ideas and between sadhaks, in order to rhythmically reel-in the Reality beyond.

8
Authentic Self-Contact

Only by becoming more aware and more conscious of the reality of the Self, will the aspirant be able to meet with those things which are Truly of God; and once an authentic Self-contact has been accomplished, to commune one day, with That Which Is God Itself.

9
Only the True, Only the Real

Only the true can get to know the True.
Only the real can get to meet the Real.

10
Shock of Silence

To go beyond the hold and hypnotism of words to the state of just Being must perforce preclude the making use of words, in order to prepare the mind for the disciplined Shock of Silence.

That is to say...

["To go beyond the hold of language and the hypnotism of words to the state of just *Being*, must perforce preclude the practice of prehended speech, phonetic utterance and lilting labialization.

«The typical, spiritual utilization of monosyllabic suprasegmental mantralization must also be prohibited.»

"For that matter, any customarily responsive, (even telepathic), form of continuant communication, including that of a calm, conceptual contemplation, must summarily, be halted."

["All of this priming, Inner deprogramming and seeming, anti-pedagogical apprenticeship to Spirituality must take place purposefully in *Intuitive Time*.

Notwithstanding, it is of eminent importance that the prelude to the above, implied "*Augmentation of Awareness*" process must be undertaken only *after* an experienced pupil has demonstrated an apt, and pure pellucidity upon the Path.

Only thereupon, may it be possible for a pupil's mind to become perfectly prepared to (properly) appropriate the TRUTH, and this through the spontaneous, *subjective shock* of a stentorian, Cosmic Silence... acting dynamically upon a greatly expanded Consciousness of SELF-Revelation."]

11
Growth and Becoming

The sadhaka grows slowly into Wisdom, but eventually becomes, the Truth.

12
The Exoteric, the Mystical & the Occult

The Exoteric, in a roundabout way, leads you eventually to the darkened entrance of the Bright Inner Path.

The Mystical, in a circular-about way, leads you spiritually to the Lighted entrance of the Clear Occult Path.

The Occult, in a spiralling-about way, leads you on through spirituality, to the Esoteric entrance of the Light of Lights, and no Path.

13
Eternally the Same

Truth and Wisdom do not just happen to Happen within the sadhak.

[Both have forever subsisted as twin Realities of GOD, and have never possessed a past, nor a present, nor a future.]

[They *Are*, and have *Been*, and will Eternally *Be* the Same, whether appropriated by someone, or not.]

14
Attach Yourself Not To Meditation

O sadhaka, attach yourself not to meditation, for that space should always remain Free.

15
Love, Wisdom & Truth

Truth simply Is.
It does not unfold, evolve, or grow.
Such also is Wisdom. And such is Love.
It is the sadhak, (rather), who unfolds, evolves, and grows into Truth, into Wisdom, and into Love.

[The sadhak himself must eventually uncover the aforementioned Sacred Treasures of God deep within himself… as he consciously learns to "relate" intuitively and correctly, to Divine Life.]

[Subsequently, it is with an ever-increasing Awareness that he catches on to the "Flaming-Reality" of *Love, Wisdom,* and *Truth,* and becomes, in his turn, "<u>caught</u>" within their strong, but tender Hold.
Then, (overwhelmed), he has naught to do, but *Be.*]

16
Deny Not the Pointing Finger

The Master's finger may point to the Sun,
But do not make of his finger the Sun.
The Sun may illuminate the finger (which points at it),
But cling not, O sadhaka, to the Lighted finger."
"And sadhak, dear sadhak, O sadhaka,
Try not to deny the Pointing-finger (nor its Occult Light),
When the Sun decides to disappear."

17
"Working For God"

Working for God is God working for you.

18
Work without God

Work without God is work without Grace.

19
To Serve

To Serve brings down a Gladness into the heart; and brings about a Lightness within the head.

20
To Love
God's Will

To love is a fine thing but to love GOD's Will is another ballgame altogether.

[Moreover, it must be played a whole Light-League away from the diamond of the small self.]

21
The Time
I Have Left

Lord, this body dies, definitely dies.

[It is dying while I live... and the time I have left... is the only time I have to find Thee, the Truth, and Me.]

22
The Kinship of Light

The Light, being everywhere present in all places and persons, makes of there, a place as Bright as here; and makes of this, (or that) stranger, a someone who is as much kin, as my brother seems mine own to Love.

23
A Pure Darkness

Until a Calmness sets upon the countryside of the mind, and a pristine and a pure darkness settles in... and absolutely nothing, that is, no thought moves... Meditation has not begun.

24
Before Death Definitely Clamps its Strong Hand

The time that spills into my space, and thereby spells out my life, is all that is available to me, to Free myself somewhere Here upon a Now... before Death definitely clamps its strong hand on me again.

25
One Little Thing

Heal me of just one little thing, O Lord... ignorance.

26
People Remain
Fast Asleep

People paradoxically persist to remain fast asleep to the opportunity of the Eternal moment which slips irreversibly by, unattended to, and unrecognized by the existing ego... which pretends pretentiously to be Awake.

27
Know This!

Loved you are. Know this. And get to work.

28
Even though the
Devil Himself

Take away, O Lord, the mask of Darkness from my face... and all things in my life, (even though difficult), will be made Well... even though the Devil himself may rise up in living vision, and strike me down.

29
Legacy of Light

Become Real, and leave to others your Legacy of Light.

30
Stress-Rest

Wrest the mask of maya from your face and *stress-rest* in the Shock of S˸ELF.

31
So'ham Sharing

The boon of Brotherhood is borne upon the sharing of the So'ham Breath.

"So-ham"... "I Am He"; "He, I Am".

32
Presto, no Problemo!

If you work always with Love, and attend to the Light-within: "Presto, no problemo!"... even though they, (the once-pesky problems), still profess to appear.

33
Windows of The Heart

Once opened by the hands of an Authentic Master, the windows of the Heart never thereafter, close their shutters.

34
Where Nothing Is

Everything is born from out of the Silence (of Being), where nothing Is.

35
Where Everything Is

Out of the Sound of Silence where everything Is... Nothing, (at last), can be born.

36
WE-*ee-ee-eee!*

One you, One me, and One God forever, make WE-*ee-ee-eee*.

37
How Many Nows Must I Kill

*S*omewhere in the now, maybe the next, I am going to die.
"Sigh, how many nows must I kill, before I am to Understand."

38
"Up With The One!"

Up with The One; down with Separation — only then, can Life un-earth you... and beguile you with Heaven's enchantment.

39
"Differences"

If you keep on seeing differences, à la droite and à la gauche, this alone will keep you away from God.

40
The Moment Is of Moment

The moment cannot be anything other than O.K. in what It Is, full of what it is, as it is, and in what it brings to you of moment, to Experience, and to Learn.

41
The Murder of Life

Killing time is murdering Life.

42
Losing Time, Wasting Time

In losing time, you lose life; in wasting time, you waste yourself.

43
To Find You Always, (O Lord)

Prepare this pilgrim, O Lord, to heed your Voice; to love You for You Alone; and to find You always in my nearest neighbour's heart.

44
Prepare this Pilgrim

Prepare this pilgrim, O Lord, to take an active part in the Plan of God for man, beast, and planet.

45
To Practice the Presence

To practice the Presence is to pin-point God as being precisely-preciously, Everywhere.

46
To Perceive Life Passionately

To live life Immediately is to perceive it passionately the moment it passes, and to perfunctorily say, Thank You.

47
How Little You Know

With the realization of how little you know, the Ocean within you, deepens.

48
No Escape

The Spiritual Path is the value of daily life duly Recognized — there is no escape upon the Way.

49
Possibility-In-God

Your possibility-in-God is impossibly Grand.

50
A Crimp in The Path

The desire for phenomenon is apt to put a personal crimp in the Path of TRUTH.

51
Through the Form

Only by Loving *through* the form can you go beyond the Form.

52
True Knowledge

True Knowledge begins when the heart gives birth to Love.

53
A Grain of Minute Rice

The approximate equivalent of a grain of minute rice, is about all you can know of the Total (cauldron of) Truth, in any one moment of Time.

54
Something & Nothing

To know something of everything about here is to know everything of nothing about There.

[Simply put: "To know *something* here is to know *nothing* about There."]

55
Keep On Knowing You Know

Keep on knowing you know, and you will just have to Love more, to finally *let go*.

56
"Concept-Caught"

If the sadhaka composes an *especial area* for the expressed emphasis of categories, (or scattergories), of thought in his Consciousness, his "Mind-self" could quite comfortably succumb to the seduction of becoming "concept-caught"; and his "Spirit-self" could subsequently, (woefully), suffer the rueful bewitchment of becoming "bodily-bound".

57
Humankind's Heart

The closer you get to GOD, the nearer you are to Humankind's Heart.

58
Blessing the Idea

When the sadhaka holds up the Ideal like a host, he blesses the Idea behind.

59
Through the Disciple's Eyes

In looking through the disciple's eyes, God sees Himself Loving everyone before Him.

60
Mirror, Mirror

Mirror, mirror on the wall, reflect not back my image, but that of God Alone... peering through my eyes, and Blessing the world with the Holy Paragate LIGHT.

61
"All Is Noodle!"

"Without experience, all is Noodle!", quips the Master.

62
A Book, Atma and Life

At best, a book on esotericism can only hint at, or inspire, a living Spirituality. [ATMA is the only True Teacher; and LIFE, the only True Guru.]

63
Spiritually-Copying

The habit of Spiritually-copying someone, (or something), is ultimately a "copping-out" vis-à-vis any serious AUTHENTICITY of *Divine Experiencing*.

64
Dream within A Dream

To chase the dream of desire, within the dream of the world, within the greater dream of Creation... is but a mere dream, within a dream, within a Dream — and none of it, Real.

65
Same Planet

Different paths, same planet, we are all pilgrims.

66
Going
« Counter-Current »

Let the unwise sadhaka keep swimming up, *(counter-current)*, to the river of Life. And unless he has developed a salmon-Sai strength, he would soon tire, and dolefully drown... *unsurrendered*, (still).

67
"The Truth
of the Depths"

To the sadhaka who has eyes to *See*, the Truth of the depths is somehow *mysteriously* scribbled upon every surface.

68
Mine is Mine

When will the nonsense of mine is mine and yours is yours, *stop* making sense?

69
"Holy-Day"

Learn to make of yourself a Holy-day to be with.

70
Not (into) This, Nor That

I must be changed into i, and i into I... not into this, nor that.

71
« Celebrate »

With the upthrust of the moment *celebrate your Being.*
With the livingness of the moment, *celebrate your Life.*
With the passing of the moment, *celebrate your Death.*

72
« All Such Phonies »

True Love loves only Real Love.

[Sentimentalism, romanticism, passion and all such phonies, fall like chaff before the blade of the Real.]

73
Two False Lovers

Sentiment and romance are the two false lovers of Love.

74
More, More, More

No matter how many times you go down upon your knees, (or sit to meditate), there is more to Realize, more to Erase, more to Understand, more to Empty.

75
A Mayfly's Prayer

Your time (upon earth) is proportionately as brief as a mayfly's prayer (for long life), cast upon the waters of desire.

76
The Grandness of His Oneness

His Name is indeed Many, so many, that a multitude and a multiplicity of varied forms and religions and messiahs... are not enough, to contain the Grandness of His Oneness.

Paradisal Plums

Second Bushel

December 14, 1991 - January 3, 1992

77
Why Ask Questions

If Love has no answers, why ask questions of Love.

78
I Was Missing...

In the beginning I was missing, till the Teacher found Me, and filled me with Life.

79
"No Matter How"

There is only one way for me to fall, no matter how, and that is into Him, more and more.

80
He Holds Me

No longer does it matter how I may falter, or fall, and suffer; or where I may scrape my being... for He Holds me.

81
The Answer

Love has no answers, It Is The Answer.

82
Free to Go

You will remain with the Master, but only when you realize that you are fully Free to go.

83
Lay Down Your Mind

Toss your world into the Great Emptiness and lay down your mind upon the grass, and with folded wings, let your Being dream the great Dream of Consciousness, filled with the Ananda of God.

84
Like the Wind

As He is there and everywhere, He is also *everything-at-once*; and like the Wind, His soft whisper calls to my Soul, and I come from *everywhere-at-once* to worship Him in everything.

85
"S & M"

Suicide is murder; murder is suicide.

86
Here-There

He is there. He is not. He is here.
Perhaps. Perhaps not.

87
The Skies of Pleasure

Like birds of prey gliding upon the winds of fatal fortune, combing the ground below for the profit of lowly carrion, there are today, too many businessmen in high positions of wealth and power who fly the skies of pleasure, and comb the world for the carrion of economic gain.

88
"For That Which Lasts"

Love that which lives, and Live for that which lasts.

89
Tornado

Become a tornado of tenderness.

90
"Tender-Talk, Tender-Walk"

Tender-talk and tender-walk your way back to God.

91
The More You Give...

Always, the more you Give, the More to you, even if you don't get.

92
"That Fire"

Breathe the love of God into everything, and that Fire will take care of petty desire.

93
"Face All Equally"

Face the big fry or the small fry equally — calmly, cooly, collectedly, and Christly.

94
For the Sake of your Spirit

As you do not place poison into the mouth, do not please, *for the sake of your Spirit*, put poison into the mind.

95
Puny Puddles

Most people do overcome with fine courage the big obstacles and the large tragedies of life, but tend to trip over the puny puddles of persistent problems that come sneaking in, upon the small moments of a day's unfolding.

96
Saints Savor...

Saints savor the sublime Ecstasy of singing the Lord's Song with their life's example.

97
Pain and Sorrow

Pain means do not touch life in this way; sorrow means do not relate to life in that way.

98
« Anguish »

Anguish is basically, the self dis-ease of an all-Relatedness avoidance.

[From another perspective, it may be seen as the egoic malaise of a fundamental evasion, vis-à-vis the Recognition of the (*Essentially* all-pervading) Relationship of the One-Self, to the all-Manifest.]

99
Give Up Your Pain

Give up your pain by giving up your self.

100
"The Brightest Bright of Them All"

The attributes of God are bright beams of Light brilliantly illuminating the night of a man's ignorance; but the brightest Bright of them all, happens when there are None at all... that is, when all such attributes are absolutely Absorbed.

101
Speeding Through Life

Speeding through life is to actually spend one's energy trying to extricate oneself from the false oppression of Time.

102
Torch of the Atman

In blowing out the candle of the self, you Light-up the torch of the Atman within.

103
Oblivion

Cry your self into *oblivion*, then Rejoice.

104
« All Things »

The *Kingly FATHER* is the Will *which empowers* all things.

The *Queenly MOTHER* is the Compassion *which loves* all things.

The *Princely SON* is the Intelligence *which moves* all things.

The *Princess DAUGHTER* is the Truth *which beautifies* all things.

The *Royal GRANDCHILD* is the Magic *which transforms* all things.

The *Imperial GREAT-GRANDCHILD* is the Grace *which transfigures* all things.

The *Future Supreme SOVEREIGN* is the Paramatman Light *which reveals* all things.

105
"If You're In the Way"

Even a spiritual pebble bonks hard, if you're in the way, and in a hurry.

106
"Experiential Moments" Slipping By

The existence, (or rather, occurrence), of Time covers up our own Existence, and makes us lose our way, as we listen to the loud ticking of our "experiential moments" slipping by... unMinded by us, and unattended to, by the *subjective core of our BEING*.

107
Whilst Time...

We pretend to be so busily occupied by time, whilst Time is scrumptuously feasting upon our (human) Soul, and burying our Being(ness) alive.

108
Disciple
vs
Ordinary Man

The disciple of Life consumes Time creatively, whilst the ordinary man is constantly being chewed up by time.

109
The Boredom-Bug

Impossible is it for the true Lover of Life to ever get the boredom-bug.

110
"Remembering Him"

By faithfully Remembering Him, you shall do ever more in the world, with even less of the world.

111
« You Shall Die »

Really, really, really believe that you shall die.

112
"Die Deeper-Down Yet"

As the sadhaka delves deeply into Meditation, all that may be darkness within, moans for the LIGHT.

As the sadhaka "dies" deeper-down yet, and shatters into Shunyata, all that was the bhoga of the flesh, (now) howls for the SPIRIT.

113
A Tap on Desire

To put a tap on Desire is to put a cap on the pain of pleasure.

114
Ever Gentler

Gentler, gentler, ever gentler in thought, speech, and action towards *man*, becomes the Lover of God.

115
Inherently Invisible

Admit it, *you* are Inherently Invisible; why do you fuss so much over the body?

116
Love activates Wisdom

To demonstrate Love is to activate Wisdom.

117
Pretty Penny

Passing pleasures cost a pretty penny for practically no profit.

118
Gift of Wings

Throw yourself into the Grand Canyon of Life and learn all about the gift of Wings.

119
Sharing

Greater is the wealth of Sharing to that of keeping.

120
Be Careful

Be careful of all things that tend to Claim you — money, sex, power, and human love.

121
Do-and-Die

You do, you die.

122
Hide-and-Seek

Pleasure and pain are all around but so is Purusha — hide-and-seek, anybody?

123
Soft-Wiring In the Mind

Lack of discipline is a kind of soft-wiring in the mind; and because of this, the mind tends to say "no" to too many of the things... which the Chalice of the Moment offers as "teaching hosts".

124
Then Be, Then Do

Forget, then Be.
Love, then Do.

125
hOMe

Roam the day with **OM**. At night, go **hOMe**.

126
Burnballs and Such Whatevers

When the pitcher throws you a curve, a hook, a sinker, a sucker-ball, or a fastball (in baseball), you catch it, and you play the game, with all you've got.

When somebody throws you a criticism, a hitch, a downer, a bait-ball, or a burn-ball (in life), you (should) also catch it, and continue to play the Game, (with all you've got).

Burnballs and such whatevers, are what oddly enough, (in their aggregate power), add up to Learning... (and are often tagged by the bat of destiny), as the burning-off, of negative karma.

[It is by these stealthy and "skillful means" of the Spirit, then, that one regains the opportunity to Purify the self; and thus, also learns to (better) work-in the leather of Life, with the mitt of Consciousness.]

127
Detachment

Detachment delights in God.

128
Man's Plan

Man's plan should always have **Ram** in hand.

129
"Hey, Don't Sway!"

Hey, don't sway, let the old ways go their lonely way.

130
With All Of Your Ear

Hear with all of your Ear the Inner Seer.

131
"Relax into God"

When relaxing, relax deeply into God.
Then raise your Inner gaze to the Kuthasta Sun,

And There, bathing in the Light of the SOUL,
LOVE *will find you*, naked and unafraid.

132
Nature of the Old

It is the nature of the old (to try) to enfold the New into its musty mold.

133
Silence of Soul

The Silence of Soul shell-shocks the Mind into the Stillness of Spirit.

134
"Ever-Fresh Ears"

If you make the effort to hear with ever-fresh ears, the ever-New will inevitably appear.

135
Child-Within

Only the original Innocence of the Child-within, can make the Holy Spirit see clearly through our eyes.

136
Every Time Its Bliss Beckons

Atman changes me every time its Bliss beckons, though my physical-sarup strangely seems to stay the same... Almost.

137
About Abutting the Void

K<small>NOWING</small> is about abutting the Void *with the mind blanking-out*, to leave a place for Reality.

138
Rise from the Sleep of Life...

The best time to rise from the sleep of life is Now, before you dream away the rest of your existence.

139
The Eventuality of Self-Realization

Do not hurry the moment of "Awakening". It will come of its own... provided that sister Srama and devi Dama, are around.

[Straightforwardly upon becoming a Disciple, the sadhaka must dutifully do what he has to do, in order to prepare his physical vahana, for the great eventuality of Self-Realization.]

[Firstly, he must become Spiritually-fit with the discipline of a steadfast sadhana.

Secondly, he must be filled with the tenderest devotion toward both God and Guru.

Thirdly, he must endeavor with all his mind, and might, and Spirit, to become... the Purely Om.

Fourthly, he must be willing to "break-Open" (his Heart) daily, in order to be tapasya-pierced by GOD's Grace.]

140
'Only Thy Oneness'

A thousand teachers have taught me ten thousand things... (regarding the Truth)... but only Thy Oneness has given It to me.

141
« Where It's At »

O sadhaka, where it's at... is *Om Tat Sat*.

142
"The Harbor of the Heart"

Soham, I am in Hridayam.

143
Listen with your Being

If you learn to Listen with all of your Being, your Heart will dispel all doubt, definitively.

144
"How can I Forget"

How can I forget what I am bound to Remember.

145
"Babbling Mind"

A mind which bubbles and babbles busies the brain and baffles the Spirit.

146
"Hoist High the Holy Host"

Hoist the Consciousness up high like a *holy host* into the sky of CREATION.

Hoist high *the hosts of thoughts* as stars into the sky of Consciousness and (dare to) twinkle for he who casts his eyes up in hope, healing, and hallowness.

147
Divine Dharma

Divine Dharma divaricates into *dedicated duty*.

Paradisal Plums

Third Bushel

January 6 - 7, 1992

148
"Proper Focus"

The one-heart of Love brings into proper focus the one-eye of Truth.

149
New-Agers

Many New-Agers write and talk as if their spiritual platitudes will one day go platinum.

150
Greatest Handicap

To think that you can make it on your own is the greatest handicap this side of Heaven.

151
Time & Space

Whilst time hypnotizes, space holds (one) in captivity.

Till time frees the self and space releases the being, the sadhaka has not Awakened.

152
To Every Spiritual Season

To every spiritual season there is a Divine Reason which seasons the sadhak.

153
Do the Walking, Without...

The Master will quietly accompany you upon the Way, but you must do the Walking without the talking.

154
The Fourth Demarcation Point

Once the Fourth demarcation point is passed, you walk the rest of the way to the Alone, alone.

155
In Striving, and Failing

In striving to conceive God, the average man fails to perceive Him.

[In striving to claim God as his own, he also fails to have Him.]

156
Quiet Crematorium

If you are not alert and careful, comfort will bury your Spirit alive.
[Comfort is the quiet crematorium of the Soul.]

157
To Keep His Peace...

Man may want to attain to God, but he also wishes to keep his peace — a Spiritually obvious, impossibility.

158
Main Muncher and #1 Killer

Moha is the main muncher of Moksha.

Corollary: (Fulfillment is the #1 killer of Freedom.)

159
The "Former Peace"

In order for the sadhaka to proceed from impermanent peace to permanent Peace, the former (temporary) peace, must often be purged and extirpated.

160
Do You Really?

Do you really want what you think you wish to have?

161
"Truckers" of the Spirit

Truckers of the Spirit are sorely needed upon God's highways.

162
Lest They Make You Forget...

Let Me protect you from your pleasures, lest they make you forget the pain of birth.

163
« Baseball Cap »

The Crown of Spiritual Leadership is often one made of thorns, but an authentically Divine Coach wears it in dignified fashion, like some sort of comfortable baseball cap.

164
"The Cloud of the World"

Wipe the "cloud of the world" from your eyes.
Let the Light of Heaven shine-on through.

165
'Strong & Sturdy'

Do drop the memory of the suffering-self, and rise up strong and sturdy, into the *Joy* of Second Birth.

166
"Within Ourselves"

Within ourselves there are things we have yet to see, places we have yet to travel, a Treasure we have yet to claim, and a Self we have yet to Be.

167
Now, Your Task...

In bringing you this far, I have done My Duty. Now, it is your task to complete the Trek, from out of the Dream begun.

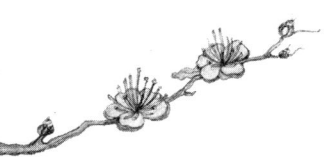

168
« Ready-Teddy »

Be a ready-teddy for the jack-in-the-box of today.

169
All-Ready Here, Already There

To be all-ready Here is to be already There without ever having left.

170
« Dissatisfaction »

Dissatisfaction is the beginning of some serious Satisfaction.

171
A Past Outdone

When the old mask weeps and the paint is peeling, the tears are usually for the eclipse of a past outdone, in looking back to one's youth... for some sort of Healing.

172
"Vidya Voyager Prajnana Porter"

Be not a time traveler but a Vidya Voyager.
Be not a soul traveller but a Prajnana Porter.

173
Corn-Flakes, Musty Grains, and Past Rains

Dislodge the encrustations of the Consciousness, clear the mind of the old corn flakes, decrystallize the brain of the musty grains, and brush-clean the canopy of Spirit, from the rust of past rains.

174
Lose & Loosen

In learning to lose, you begin to win; in learning to loosen, you begin to gain.

175
"The Soul Moves Not..."

The Soul moves not, but Is.

[This Isness is projected into *subjective* space wearing the overcoat of *objective* time; and dies in the *becoming* of the body, transpierced by the St. Sebastian of substance.]

176
"Everywhere Sibilant"

Whether in the cave, the monastery, the woods, or the city — the Song of the Soul is everywhere sibilant.

177
Be No One

Be no one but yourself *being* your Self.

178
Imitate No One

Imitate no one but your Self imitating no one.

179
Somewhere, Somehow

The newborn babe has that power to stir Awake within the mom and dad of everyone "the Little Child"... who somewhere, somehow, got lost.

180
"His Gaze"

When God flashes His gaze into the Heart of a man, Brightness is the result.

181
"Open" Spaces

God sprinkled Liberty liberally into the little and the big "Open" spaces of His creation.

182
A Moment In Eternity

A moment in Eternity can only happen when the eyes are Open.

183
Splicing
the In-Between

To see through the Middle is to splice the in-between into two halves that don't exist.

184
« Snowflaking »

Giving Glory to God always snowflakes upon your head.

185
"And Make my Motor Hum..."

Grease me with your Grace, God, lube me good with your Spirit, empower me with your Will, and make my motor hum... to your Love Alone.

186
"All God's Attributes"

If out of all God's attributes Love is said to be His Glory, then His Will must surely be the Crown.

187
"In the Human Heart"

Love came out of God's Bosom and found its home in the human heart.

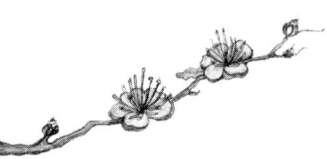

188
"Correctly Discerning"

Correctly discerning between the good and the bad makes for the (almost) straight Path.

189
When the World is Wrong, and our Sadhana is Lacking

The world is wrong when our thinking is wrong; our sadhana is lacking when our Spirit is lacking.

190
« Keeping It So »

Our Inner world being essentially good, our job is to keep it so, with right thought.

191
An Ongoing Detachment

An ongoing Detachment from both the good and the bad, eventually frees you from the Path.

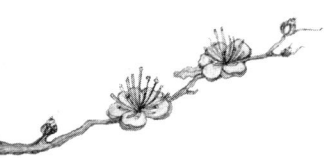

192
"Thoughts Go Astray"

Thoughts go astray before a man does.

193
Self-Interest

Self-interest is a blight upon humanity's capacity to demonstrate Love.

194
Ephemeral Man, Enduring Man

Ephemeral man tends to choose the unreal; the enduring man always chooses the Real.

195
Sin & Scruples

A lack of scruples leads to the lack of the perception of sin.

196
Simple Pride
Spiritual Pride

The danger of simple pride is common delusion.
The danger of spiritual pride is Divine delusion.

197
Altruism

Altruism is too often assessed by self-interest.

198
Real Love

Real Love is too often measured by the rule of self-love.

199
True Vision

True Vision fades as egoism cataracts the single Eye.

200
Modern Malady

The ubiquitous nonchalance and the apparent non-caring for that which is enduring and Eternal... is simply symptomatic of the malady of modern man's immeasurable miasmic narcissism.

201
Spiritual Alchemy

Spiritual Alchemy is the Mind converting bad into Good; and the Spirit metamorphosing evil into Virtue.

202
« Deliberately-Bad »

Deliberately-bad shortens your life, not to say that it is "painfully-contractive" to the Spirit.

203
"Self-Love" and "Ordinary Ego"

Fill-up with the common fuel of "self-love" and your cosmic Cardiac-converter gets cheated-out of the high-grade essence of Real LOVE.

Fill-up with the cheap fuel of "ordinary ego" and your Being's main motor mournfully loses the purlful Hum of the Soul.

204
Deal & Cope

The sadhaka deals with the adverse of joy and sorrow similarly to the way he copes with the extremes of heat and cold.

205
"Puff"

Puff yourself up with pride, power, and position... and *puff* goes your Spirit.

206
The Plain
of the Mind

Between joy and sorrow, pain and pleasure, and all such opposite poles, stretches the meandering plain of the mind... with its endless wheat fields of (positive and negative), swaying thought.

207
The Mode
of the Mind

The mode of the mind molds matter into the mattering of the world.

208
« Lofty Mind,
Lowly Mind »

The *lofty mind* sails forth upon the high winds of Spirit to gather and to cull from our glorious Creation the golden nuggets of apperceived Good.

The *lowly mind* sets out into the storm of Life brimming with fire and brimstone, and quickly runs amuck, amongst the black shoals of many unperceived Evils.

(The mind slips hither and thither to gather Good... or to wither.)

209
The Greater Good, (Always)

True Spiritual discipline is choosing the greater good, (always).

210
Tests & Trials

Without the tests and the trials the value of Life diminishes to an almost *personal* none.

211
Without Bad, Without Hate

Without Bad, who would ever go looking for good.
Without Hate, who would ever (even) desire love.

212
« Truth-Touching »

The Self in you touches the Self in me.

[Concentrate upon this Truth-touching, and all things will connect rightly.]

213
(Spiritual)
Non-Action

Refine the sword of the Self to a fine cutting edge, strong in the constant practice of (spiritual) Non-action.

214
Toil & Trouble

Toil and trouble tend to force us to face life with the spear and the shield of our Inner Spirit raised.

Toil and trouble tend to thrust us forward to find an even greater meaning to Existence and Evolution.

Toil and trouble tend to make of us, through conflict and the courageous conquering of all those forces opposing us... seasoned, Spiritual Warriors.

Jaya! Jaya!

215
'Walking the Line of Impeccability'

Without the potentially challenging power of those life situations which offer a natural healthy "opposition" to all of us, none of anything in life, would be in the least bit interesting, nor even "attractive".

[The kinetically-karmic, lila-linking of the right side to the left side of everything in the honing Light of humility, humor, and kindness is the warrior-like line of Impeccability in both deed and thought that the disciple must walk.]

[By means of the discipline inherent in his Sadhana's quest, the disciple's aim is to attain simultaneously an open, fluid, *worldly* Equilibrium... paralleled with the (tricky) achievement of a stable, yet (always) "radical" *spiritual* Equanimity.]

216
Uneasiness of the World

The uneasiness of the world lies in the attachment of the mind to that which is unessential, and ephemeral.

217
Interchanging "Self-Interest"

By sagely interchanging self-interest for Self-interest, the sadhaka slowly and seriously, sets himself upon the Way.

218
In Being Neither-Nor

The 'I am this', or 'I am that' viewpoint, is nullified by the 'I am not this', or 'I am not that' position.

[It is only in being "neither-nor" that all comparison collapses, all competition crashes, all discord disappears, and all differences are resolved into Oneness... and it is only after having attained this perspective that the Divine Sameness "within-differences", can thereupon be addressed, with the utmost of Love and Respect.]

219
...Then Meditate

Disperse the bad, cremate the negative, purify your mind, sanctify your life, then Meditate.

220
Artificiality

Artificial means not-real... how Real are you?

221
Banish to Nether-Netherlands

Banish to nether-netherlands:
a)   the binding up of Life with likes and dislikes;
b)   the enslaving of the Self with the desire for this, or the desire for that;
c)   the cramming of the Consciousness with either good, or bad;
d)   the obsession of the Spirit with either union, or separation.

If the sadhak applies himself assiduously to the above:
a)   *the Pearl of Power, eventually appears.*
b)   *the Crown of Compassion, incarnates.*

222
Valueless Meditation

To meditate with a lie festering in your mind is next to valueless.

223
"Meditative Plasticism"

Plastic meditation comes out of a plastic heart.

224
Scrumptious God-Nutrition

Spiritual food is scrumptious God-nutrition — whether sweet, or sour.

225
"Faking"

You can fake meditation but you cannot fake your Self.

226
'Doing Japa'

You may pretend that you do Japa but you cannot make Japa Do you.

227
« Equal Gratitude »

All that happens to us is the product of one's own actions and thoughts, past and present.

None of it issues from God, except His Grace.

[Therefore, do not raise your spiritual fist in anguish, nor in righteousness towards God... for what may *seem* to be going wrong in your sadhana, or within your life.]

[Accept with equal gratitude the seemingly good and the seemingly bad.]

[What issues "transformatively" out of both the positive and the negative in one's life is one's Jivatmic prerogative... and of course, one's Divine *Atmic* responsibility.]

228
Daily Duties

All daily duties are to be placed at the feet of God with Love.

229
In the Interim...

The SELF is the Real: *you* are only there in the interim.

230
Waste of Life

Since dead is not Dead, mourning for the dead is generally a *waste of Life*.

231
One Fine, Divine Delusionary Day

The undertaking of the Spiritual life is an endless voyage toward both Self-hood and God-hood... (the two "hoods" which we must, one fine, Divine delusionary day, rip away from our Naked FACE).

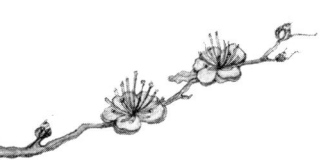

232
« Dollar Evolution »

Sad is dollar evolution without Spiritual revolution.

233
Share It

Money in flow is money on the go; let it ride, let it ride!

[Give it, sow it, spend it, *Share it* — if you let it go with a selfless flair, and with an acute "awaring" of the fundamental flow *(of the Law of Abundance)*, plenty of it there will always be.]

234
Do Not Cling, Do Not Cloy

To cling to possessions is to doubt God; to cloy to money is to dump Him.

235
Like Milk, It Will Curdle

Do not let money stand still; like milk, it will curdle, go bad, taste sour, and turn on you.

236
Worthless Wealth

Rich in money, (without rich in God), is a worthless wealth.

237
Helping The Needy

Helping the needy is an absolute necessity of honest money.

238
Bless Others With It

If you are blessed with money, bless others with it.

239
Giving $

Money generously given out goes *gleefully gonging* into GOD's glove.

Money charitably handed out *falls fatefully* into HARI's Hand.

Money heaped holistically upon the needy and helpless magically becomes HARIDHANA, *(the true treasure of Vishnu)*.

240
Wherever Poor Is...

Wherever poor is, (in the flesh, or in the spirit), *there...* do give of your Wealth.

241
To the Poor...

To the poor a dollar is Purusha in the palm.

242
To the Hungry...

To the hungry a dollar is Brahma in the belly.

243
Immediately Rich

Lovingly let go of money and you are immediately rich in Something other.

244
Desire & Use

The only problem there may be with money is in the how much you *desire* it, and in the way you make *use* of it.

245
God's Wealth

Man's Love is God's *real* wealth.

246
Love of Money

Love of money distorts Love and sadly disowns Divinity.

247
Shootin' & Rootin'

Learn to earn your money shootin' straight, shootin' high, and shootin' for God... while rootin' for man.

248
Easy Bonfire

If you constantly accumulate money, or get caught by the dollar-(POWER) sign... then the matches, (or *the sulfurous experiences*) of life, will make an easy bonfire of you.

249
"Give & Gain"

God gave all away and gained Creation.

250
Greatest Gift
of the Dollar

The greatest gift of the dollar is in the lending of a helping hand for the eventuation of God's Plan.

251
Greatest Return
of a Dollar

The greatest return of a dollar correctly spent is in the (delightful) incurring of the Soul's Blessing.

252
These Same...

Christ Loved the poor, He gave of Himself to them, and these same, Loved Him.

253
"It Ain't Yours, Babe"

"All of the money of the world resides in God's bank... and *it ain't yours, Babe!*"

254
$-Symbol

Money magnetizes itself into a free-swirl of charitable work around the Spiritual Master who has attuned himself to the true significance of the $-symbol.

255
Materiality and Mastership

Money, (and materiality), should swirl about a Master, as the winds of a hurricane, swirl around a still centre.

256
Rich in God

He who is rich in GOD has a PROVIDENTIAL bank account Everywhere.

PARADISAL PLUMS

FOURTH BUSHEL

JANUARY 8 - 11, 1992

257
In Step

With the mastership of the Self the environment will always move in step.

258
Eight Sacred "Self-Recognitions"

As the sadhaka moves forward in Spiritual unfoldment, his subjective outlook and overall attitude regarding LIFE undergo constant change, until finally, all rules, (and even laws), attendant to mortality, cease to be... since they are all absorbed, (one by one), into a series of *eight* sacred SELF-Recognitions, leading first to a "Fusion-with-Guru" and ultimately, to a "Union with GOD".

SR-1
Subjective Mastery

SELF-Recognition I: As the sadhaka moves ever closer to a Subjective Mastery (of Life), the SOUL which he both already Is and is Divinely-Becoming, stirs more sensitively "awake" within all of his kosas, or bodies.

SR-2
Better Comprehension
Fresh Apprehension

SELF-Recognition II: The sadhaka, thereafter, begins to better Comprehend and to freshly Apprehend, the esoteric subtleties of LIFE's evolutionary processes.

SR-3
More Mindfulness

SELF-Recognition III: The sadhaka expediently exhumes and examines with a mite more Mindfulness (and personal might), the Spirit-animated, teeming multitude... of LIFE's multi-level states of Consciousness.

SR-4
No End of Happiness

SELF-Recognition IV: The sadhaka appreciates to no end of Happiness the manifestly-variegated Infinity of both the actual and possible "FORM-*expressions*" of Existence.

259
Love Sees Beyond

Love takes in the Whole of the all of it and sees beyond diminutive judgement.

SR-5
Overflowing Joy

Self-Recognition V: The sadhaka realizes with a Heart full of suddenly-found Contentment, that all of the above subjective Self-unfoldings were in their *Soul-ar activity*, enigmatically-tinged <u>all the while</u>, with a certain inner constancy of overflowing JOY.

SR-6
Sacred Awe and
Divine Spontaneity

Self-Recognition VI: A new, authentic Sacred Awe presently instills itself in the sadhaka vis-à-vis the always natural, surprisingly Radical, and yet, formidably precise demonstration of "Divine Spontaneity"... which he (now) *Sees*, as being actively "eloquent" everywhere... and which "mysteriously" <u>underscores</u> the all of Creation.

SR-7
The Divine Drop
and the Ocean of Love

Self-Recognition VII: The sadhaka Becomes the OM'd Breath, the Bodhichitta Heart, the Divine Drop, the Salted-SELF, dropped into the LORD's *Ocean of LOVE*.

SR-8
Compassion and
the Orange Palm

Self-Recognition VIII: Drenched in COMPASSION, the new BUDDHA *spontaneously* lifts his right hand from out of the Earth's pain, and with an Open *Orange* Palm, blesses the All-in-All within the Living WHOLE... in the Sacrosanct *(Sweet)* Name of the SILENT WATCHER... Who rests Eternally in the HEART of (every man's) Heart.

260
Law of the Realized

The law of the Spirit is *the only law* of the REALIZED.

261
« Rules Rule »

Rules rule the lower nature... as they help align the self to one's *possibility-in-God*.

262
Rules and Regulations

Rules, regulations, methods, techniques, observations, and discipline are for those who have *not yet Attained* (to God).

263
Law of the Land, Law of the Spirit

For the Saint, the law of the land and the Law of the Spirit, go hand-in-hand, even in difference.

264
« Gross to God »

The Guru goads you from gross, to Grace, to Glory, to God.

265
Silence of Selfhood, & Buddhic Ambiguity

"The Silence of SELFHOOD summons forth the simple song of the Saint with an ecstatic Spontaneity.

[That is to say, the Buddhic, intuitive faculty of the Soul aligned to the Divine Will, (or Spiritual Intention), is the primary and Only Motivator of the *modus vivendi* of the Mystic.]

[That is to say, Buddhic Ambiguity collimated to Christly WILL is the causal channel of conduct for the confirmed Occultist.]

266
Practice of Viveka

If something "appeals" to the sadhaka, it is considered the proper practice of "Viveka" on his part, to spot-check on just how much of it is impurely due to his *ego*... gross or subtle, being attracted.

267
"Tune-In" to Eternity

You can tune-in to Eternity whilst travelling through time, but you can only do so upon the Tone of Truth.

268
Jesus Crossed Heaven

Jesus crossed Heaven upon the Cross of Christ.

269
A Master Spirit

Only when a Master Spirit has prevailed and spraddled the Path all the way to PURUSHA, can he then with perfect poise and poignant prajna, point the Way.

270
A Thousand and One

A thousand teachers, (acharyas, arhats), make up a Guru.

A thousand gurus make up a Sant Satguru; 1001, a Satguru.

A thousand Satgurus make up an Authentic Master of Wisdom:
- a Jnana Param Satguru,
- a Prajnana Param Satguru.

A thousand Param Satgurus make up a Paraparam Adept:
- an Amitabha Buddha,
- a Maitreya Buddha,
- a Poorna Avatara,
- a Maha Avatara,
- a Purusha Jnani,
- a Paraparam Prajnani.

271
The One

Gods, goddesses, and gurus may be seen, felt, or experienced; but The ONE Is simply, *Beyond the Beyond*.

272
Guruship

Guruship is making God the Guru and Life the Teacher.

273
« Steed of Sri Guru »

Hop the steed of Sri Guru, and reap the wild Wind of the Spirit.

274
Gnana Guru

A Gnana Guru gets your heart a'flutterin' and sets your Soul a'tremblin'.

275
God "Angling"

A Guru is God *angling* for a disciple.

276
The Zero

Ten thousand selves make up the *zero* of the selfless Self.

277
Need for Illumination, Reason for Realization

The primary need for Illumination is to provide a Light-source for the sake of others.

(The real reason for Realization is to liberate the Living Light from out of the Egg of SELF.)

278
An Open, Vulnerable Heart

The sadhaka's correct consumption of Compassion from a Satguru requires, *(from the point of view of a disciple's allegiance)*, the uncompromising condition of an open, Vulnerable Heart.

279
Best Way

To put the whole of yourself in thought upon the Guru-within is the best way to Silence the world.

280
« Stick 'em Up! »

Guruship is Surrendership.

281
Mind Din

Mind agitation is Self-frustration and Guru-exasperation.
Mind intrusion is Self-interruption and Guru-exacerbation.

282
So Sure &
So Pure

There is nothing so *sure* and so *pure* as the Guru's gaze upon your Heart.

283
"Any Cup"

The Guru's Grace fills any cup whatever the size that is brought. The only condition is an *undefiled Sincerity*.

284
Impact of a Guru

If you wish to reduce the impact of a Guru upon you, get more familiar, more personal, more self-conscious, more self-reliant, and more self-willed... that should do it.

285
Guru's Glance

The glance of the Guru is God's coup de Grâce.

286
Guru's Gaze

The gaze of the Guru is the slayer of the false in you.

287
God Looking Out, God Speaking Out

What comes out of the eyes of a Guru is GOD looking out through LOVE's Shining.

What comes out of the mouth of a Guru is GOD speaking out with LOVE's Promise.

288
Constantly Kind

How constantly kind is the mind of a Master.

289
Altitude-Attitude

Switch the personal attention to the Pure Consciousness of the SOUL, knowing that It is permeating all, watching all, Being all, and Loving all.

[This "Altitude-Attitude" alone should in the long run release you to know both God and Grace, *here* and *now*.]

290
Desiring Desire

Don't give up on the world, nor give up the world... for you are in it only for the duration that you desire Desire... and remain attached to, (or identified with), that which is desired.

291
Pushing Right, Pulling Left

Desire pushes the mind right to creatively fashion, and desire pulls the mind left to creatively destroy.

292
Detachment from Desire

Detach yourself decidedly from desire and even Death will back off.

293
Brink of Madness

Desire is in the main a pseudo-expansive, (and an emotionally-expensive), attitude which drives the minds of men often to the brink of madness within the contractive shell, (or the prison-cell), of the ego.

294
Layer by Layer

Peel your self gently away from desire, layer by layer, as with an onion, and in due course, you will experience the CENTRE — Pure Potentiality, enfolded by Kinetic Nothing(ness).

295
Desire Minus you, Desire Plus you

Desire minus you = DETACHMENT, leading to → *Dispassion*.
Desire plus you = ATTACHMENT, leading to → *Impassion*.

296
Whom Desire Cannot Shove, & Cannot Bully

Calm is he whom desire cannot shove.
Content is he whom desire cannot bully.

297
Lightly & Soundly

With a passionate Fire but with no driving desire, the sadhaka rides *Lightly* and *Soundly*, in the saddle of Life.

298
Small "d" to Big "D"

The small "d" standing in for the desires of creation must one day give way to the big **"D"** of **D**esire for the **D**ivine.

Desire for the Divine, as represented by the following few examples:

A Desire for **D**A *delineating* the Father Principle
A Desire for **D**I *delineating* the Mother Principle
A Desire for **D**ADA *delineating* the Elder Brother (on the Path)
A Desire for **D**IDI *delineating* the Elder Sister (on the Path)
A Desire for **D**ADI *delineating* ½ Shiva, ½ Shakti; Male/Female
 as One; (Ardhanarishvara)

A Desire for **D**AYA *depicting* Divine Compassion, Incarnate
A Desire for **D**AMA *depicting* Self Control; Real Restraint
A Desire for **D**ANA *depicting* Genuine Generosity; Sacred Charity
A Desire for **D**HARANA *depicting* Sacred Concentration
A Desire for **D**HAIRYA *depicting* Steadfastness and Courage

299
If You Must Desire

If you must desire, desire the Christ;
His Crown is the operculum of desire.

Small "d" to Big "D"

A Desire for **D**EVA *embodying* the God Radiant

A Desire for **D**EVI *embodying* the Goddess Who Shines

A Desire for **D**EVA-**M**ANDIRA *embodying* the "Abode of God"

A Desire for **D**HYANA *embodying* Deep Meditation, (where Divinity blends with the DIVINE)

A Desire for **D**HARMA *embodying* The Way (of righteous Living), or Divine Duty

A Desire for **D**AHARA *eliciting forth* the Awakening of the Heart Lotus

A Desire for **D**ARSHANA *eliciting forth* a Vision of the Sacred; or the Sighting of a Holy Man

A Desire for **D**ISPASSION *eliciting forth* a detachment in action; an impartiality; being neither for, nor against

A Desire for **D**ISCIPLINE *eliciting forth* a steady adherence to personal sadhana and to one's chosen Spiritual Path

A Desire for **D**ISCIPLESHIP *eliciting forth* the Way of Service, (in working for GOD, HIERARCHY & MAN, *impersonally*)

A Desire for **D**ATTATREYA *betokening* the Deified Incarnation of the combined energies of Brahma, Vishnu & Shiva, *(being in Hindu Mythology, the three Brothers of Creation)*, into a single concentrated form of ADEPTSHIP

A Desire for **D**AKSHINAMURTI *evoking* the Universal Teacher

300
A Killer

The last Desire, that for GOD, is a real killer.

301
The Death of One Desire

Even the death of one desire only, amazingly lightens the Spirit.

302
Sacred Cobra

You cannot destroy Desire but you can, (with Aware practice), learn to peel-off its false snake-skin.

[In time, this "ego-peeling" will activate the Sacred Cobra within, whose progressively "uplifting" Presence will both (discreetly) disclose, and (uprightly) protect, your BUDDHA Nature.]

303
Whoosh!

Your Soul-Flame must be strong and must not tremble, even when a hurricane of desire whooshes by.

304
Creative Craving

Desire is a creative *craving* for that which always disappears.

305
Who "I Am"

If I am not (my desire for) this, nor (for) that, then I must learn to rely, not on <u>what</u> I am (identified with), but on <u>Who</u>, "I Am".

306
Brink of Godhood

On the brink of Godhood, desire will fall of its own (gravity) into the Great Abyss, where even the wish to be One-with-God, will simply vanish.

307
"Dream-Dust"

Desire is the dream-dust of Divine-doings in the dark.

308
A Bottle, or
A Barrel

Cap off *desire*: keep it down to a bottle, instead of a barrel.

309
Touch But Once

Touch but once to the Silence, and *desires* will forever stop their incessant mewlings.

310
Only at First

The Way is truly desireless... and only at first, worldly-dull.

311
More and More

One day the world desired, and it has never stopped... *desiring* more and more things to desire.

312
Lost Meditation

If the mind moves, you've lost meditation — desire has disturbed it.

313
Become a Master

Master desire before it masters you;
master desire, and become a Master.

314
Make it a Habit

Masters make it a habit of desiring nothing, and of detaching themselves from even less than that.

315
The Nature of Desire

Mystics love desiring God and suffering for It — for such is the nature of desire — you suffer.

316
Important Step

An important step toward Freedom is losing the gumption to gain, and abating the desire to win.

317
A Growing Circumference
vs
No Circumference At All

Desire boasts a growing circumference, because of bigger and bigger wants and needs.
Desirelessness claims no circumference at all, for there is no want, nor need.

318
Desire and
Desirelessness

Desire *divides*... it leads to DUALITY.
Desire *adds*... it leads to ADDICTION.
Desire *differentiates*... it leads to (separative) DISCRIMINATION.
Desire *diverts*... it leads to DEVIATION.
Desire *distracts*... it leads to DELUSION.
Desire *disappoints*... it leads to DESPAIR.

DESIRELESSNESS *divulges* (the Divine)... it leads to DELIVERANCE.

319
Manna-Child

Desire married God and made manifest Man, Its Manna-Child.

320
Do More for Man

Desire less, dream less, declare less, and do more for man… with the Divine devouring every deed.

321
Quiet Corner

In a quiet corner of Nowhere lay your desires to rest, and only be Absent; and let the whole wide worried world weave, whirl, whimper, whine and whoosh away.

322
Delusionary Dilemma

Desirelessness seems to modern man an impossible state: that is, until he truly discovers the Delusionary Dilemma of the Dream.

[Only subsequently, will he set about to either *renounce*, or *re-organize* the ever-renascent "relative reality" which has so caught-up, and crazed, his Consciousness.]

323
Successful Switch-Hitting

To *adaptively*, (and successfully), switch-hit in Consciousness from the lower-self to the Higher Self, the in-training sadhaka must learn to skillfully clout the ball of desire with the bat of Renunciation, (almost every time).

324
Desire-Jump,
Desire-Dump

Desire-jump this planet, desire-jump the next world, desire-jump all dimensions, *and desire-dump desire.*

325
Achin' & Pinin' & Hangin' Dry

Solar-plexus desire, whether for things, for power, for bliss, or for God, will always leave you pinin' and hangin' dry, and with an anxious achin' in the Heart.

326
The Cross of Matter

The last Great Renunciation can only be taken up upon the Cross of Matter... mattering no more.

327
Some Beneficent Someone...

Look within, or look without... and realize that which can be described as being at the core of all sacred, Spiritual endeavor is but the Desire-body of some beneficent someone sowing his saintly Suchness... in an absolutely innocuous, sweet-state of Divinely-intentioned, self-Forgetfulness.

328
« Sweet Yuck »

Cloying to Bliss is sweet Yuck.

329
A Bald Eagle

Soar boldly as a Bald Eagle over the desert of desires.

330
"Sudden-Caught"

Let Spirit slip into the molasses of desire and its wings are sudden-caught.

331
Only One Thing...

There is only one thing that gets lost when desires disappear — your limitations.

332
"Pontifically Stuck"

By all means, do see the superb sights of the Spirit, but don't get pontifically stuck in mystical splendiferousness.

333
Even to...

The S<small>ELF</small> never has the desire to cling or cloy to anything — even to Bliss.

334
"Silly-Caught"

A spiritual desire coheres (the sadhaka) to a sticky-spot of "trapped" Consciousness... somewhat comparable to a pious fly, *silly-caught*, to some piece of mystical flypaper.

335
Don't Stop!

Flip those wings, Baby, and don't stop, even for a tempting drink of Supra-nectar.

336
Totally Trust

Totally trust that Life is more desirous of meeting your essential needs than you may know how.

337
Real Saints Don't Do That!

The sadhaka may be tempted to stay... or he may have the desire to linger at a particular (Inner) spiritual site... (or to dally in a particularly Blissful state of consciousness)... but *real Saints don't do that!*

338
Keep-on-Going, Keep-on-Doing

One giant step back and two baby steps forward... do not count, just keep-on-going on with Sadhana, and keep-on-doing your (Divine) duty.

339
Let

Let the Lord... Desire for you.

340
"What to Do?"

Which do you desire more, Love or God?
What do you want more, Desire or Divinity?

[What to do, what to do!?]

341
When the Time Is Right

Saints say that when the time is right, "desire" will fall of its own dead weight... and wrong desire(s), first.

342
"Carpet of Fire"

Resistance to desire provides the "carpet of fire" necessary for our Spirit to walk upon, towards God.

343
Rejoice Now!

Buddha struggled and attained to Buddha-hood with but the greatest of difficulty.

[This constant struggling with desire, and this continuous suffering through all of the desire-lokas, is ours, and everyone's earthly lot.]

[Occultly-speaking however, as aspiring probationers upon the Path, we could very well begin the mysterious process of "Rejoicing" now — for all of this self-inflicted, "self-desired" suffering over Desire, is ineluctably destined to lead each one of us, to his own Bodhi tree.]

344
The Work

The Work must never be a burden, nor a suffering, nor a sacrifice.

345
Confront

Confront the enemy and create the Path.

346
"Martyrs Must Sacrifice One Significant Thing"

The world's martyrs must sacrifice one significant thing in their daily life before making a serious step forward in Spirit, and that is... their *suffering*.

347
'For Heaven's Sake'

Fire, Fire within, burn me to hell, and back again... for Heaven's sake.

348
Inimical

Complaint is inimical to the Lord of Suffering.

349
"Meeting a Sage"

If a vegetarian meets a Sage, he checks the Seer's food plate, and checks out the Fool's Soul-platter.

If a philosopher meets a Sage, he plumbs the Seer's mind, and sounds out the Fool's logic.

If an astrologer meets a Sage, he surveys the Seer's signs, and charts-in the Fool's stars and planets.

If a businessman meets a Sage, he delves into the Seer's assets, and digs up the Fool's liabilities.

If a scientist meets a Sage, he examines the Seer's theories, and investigates the Fool's facts.

If a prostitute meets a Sage, she looks over the Seer's body, and assesses the Fool's sexual propensity.

If a burglar meets a Sage, he runs his eye over the Seer's material goods, and estimates the Fool's worth.

If a teacher meets a Sage, he verifies the Seer's erudition, and inquires of the Fool's education.

If a psychologist meets a Sage, he probes the Seer's psyche and analyzes the Fool's persona.

If a metaphysician meets a Sage, he peruses the Seer's precepts, and perscrutates the Fool's principles and laws.

→

350
« Corrected, Not Cracked »

"Do correct me Lord, but don't make me crack."

[Let the sadhaka stand corrected, not cracked, in Consciousness.]

"Meeting a Sage"

If a mathematician meets a Sage, he studies the Seer's theorems, and trigometrizes the Fool's sacred Triangle.

If a statistician meets a Sage, he graphs-in the Seer's everything, and predicts the Fool's popularity at the spiritual polls.

If a priest meets a Sage, he estimates the Seer's sainthood, and appraises the Fool's authority.

If a mystic meets a Sage, he scans the Seer's aura, and assays *intuitively* the Fool's vibrations.

If an occultist meets a Sage, he takes specific stock of the Seer's occultness, and secretly sets the Fool's initiation-(level).

If a moralist meets a Sage, he scrutinizes the Seer's cultivation, and *righteously* monitors the Fool's (better-be), impeccable conduct.

If a cynic meets a Sage, he disputes the Seer's sincerity, and cross-interrogates the Fool's Inspirational genius.

If a skeptic meets a Sage, he tests the Seer's objectivity, and cross-questions the Fool's authenticity.

If a Saint meets a Sage, he compassionately envisions the Seer's sins, and blesses the Fool's pretension.

Lord, what a waste! We see through what we believe we are and think we know.

351
Obscuration

The "object" of desire ever seeks to obscure the "nature" of desire.

352
True Service

True Service is beyond all sense of self-consciousness, (or sacrifice); if this is not clearly so, then the said service hides within its folds, a modicum of (undisclosed) martyrship.

353
Gently, but Gently

The untrained Spirit is corroded with self-desire; gently, but gently, brush off the samsaric rust.

354
The "Ego-Egg"

Go firmly but easy upon the ego and its desires — do not crack the "ego-egg" too soon... that is, not before it has been slowly and adequately boiled... under the proper Divine fire.

PARADISAL PLUMS

FIFTH BUSHEL

JANUARY 12 - 16, 1992

355
To Ponder upon God

To ponder upon God is eventually to become *Divine*.

356
"Broodings"

Brood upon Brahman and *Be*.
Brood upon Brahma and *Become*.

357
Blissful Baba & the Blessed Buddha

Brood upon Blissful Baba and Be BLESSED.
Brood upon Blessed Buddha and Be BLISSED.

358
Be-hood

Be-hood is built upon the broken bones of the ego.

359
« See the Best »

The ability to see the best in other is always dependent upon the capacity to see the best in oneself.

360
« Easily Cut Down »

The man who has been weakened by desire is easily cut down by Death.

361
Blasted by Desire

Blasted by desire, the blow of Death is a blessing to the being.

362
...Unless They Have Known

The gods cannot be Freed unless they have known man becoming Divine.

363
'Hard to Spot...'

The Living Lord lives within the living body — it's just hard to spot the One Life, when both are living Together.

364
Gift of Self

The greatest gift is Self given away.

365
Feet of a Guru

The FEET of a Real Guru are rooted in God's Grace.

366
Look of a Guru

The LOOK of a Real Guru is always a deluge of Light.

367
"Yog"

The Yoke of God within the Egg of Creation is to be gotten by *Yog*.

368
"Communion"

Communion — Oneness with the Divine — is predicated upon a deep, Silent communication.

369
"Siddhis" and Stepping on the Gas

A crash-course to God via the accelerated mediumship of an astral clairvoyance, or clairaudience, or via the encouragement and accomplishment of "siddhi" powers, (or through any other spiritualistic or mediumistic means), can be somewhat likened to a sadhaka stepping on the gas in order to hurry it up towards God... with his car jacked-up high on a holy hoist.

370
« Speeding Things Up »

The Black Forces always like speeding things up... to *beyond* a person's readiness point.

371
Cornmeal

Ceremony, contemplation, concentration, and meditation, as well as all other approaches to God, are for the turning of the mind into *cornmeal* for the Divine.

372
"Beautify your Life"

Before age befalls the body, bend your mind to God, and mend your way toward Truth.

[Beautify your life with the *translucent* Light of the Soul and fill your attendant days with the *fiery* Sibilance of the Spirit.]

373
Too Late

Old and weak is usually too late, at best difficult, for God to be fully Known.

374
Train and Attain
Now

*T*rain and *Attain* now while you are young and strong.

[In old age, regretfully, an untrained mind and an unattained Spirit, too often bespeak of the downfall of the Divine, before death.]

375
"Happy to Be Alive"

The body is blissfully happy to be alive. *Are you?*

376
"Wee-Words" of Woe

Two doe-eyed wee words of woe, woo wildly and without surcease, the "la dame sans merci" of desire: MORE and AGAIN.

377
"Karmic Sizzle"

Every human being is born into this world bearing the karmic sizzle of the law of "action-and-reaction" unto his incarnational flesh. None can escape it.

[Because of this *karmic branding* at Birth, to abandon, or to evade "action" remains forever an incarnational impossibility.]

[But to abandon the wish (or aversion) for a particular affect or product, as an "outcome" of action is, on the other hand, karmatically-liberating.]

378
Sri Karta's Karmaless Hands

Move and do, because move and do, *we must*.

[*Wisdom-in-doing* keeps an open Heart always, and remembers the Lord, and loves our neighbour because he is our very Self.]

[*Wisdom-on-the-move* cares not for the consequence of move-and-do, and when such a one goes *mindfully* along, he puts it all *in trust* into Sri Karta's karmaless Hands.]

379
Mere Replicas

All holy temples are mere replicas of the Body-Template.

380
The Body Too

The body too must be taken into Divine Consciousness.

381
The Pinda Kosa

Without the pinda kosa, there would definitely be no "you", down here.

[Now is the proper time to recognize the *physical* body's Divine importance.]

382
Book of Life

The law of cause and effect, that is, of "Karmic Consequence", takes notice, registers, and indeed affects every single, gross or subtle movement in the universe — even to that of an entire planet, a single mind, a simple thought, a collective consciousness; or to the complex convolutions of curving light, and of cosmic sounds.

[All vibrational, gyrational, small and great glyphs, whether of a personal, or of a universal nature, are neatly, correctly, impeccably, and unremittingly scribed into the Book of Life.]

[Ah, the Wonder!]

383
'Never As Rewarding'

Emptying the pockets of the addictive ownership of possessions can never be as rewarding as emptying the self... of the addictive possessorship of *self-interest*.

384
Private Chamber

The only place to look for the Lord of Love is within His Private Chamber — the HEART.

385
The Dark-Blue Cavern

Going to the "heart of something" means attaining to that specific area which is of a "centremost" depth — and so it is within man.

[Spiritual man must turn the attention of his Consciousness inwards to the specific area of the Heart-Plexus near the spinal column; it is only there, in the deepermost exploration of the *Dark-Blue Cavern*, that he will find the Christ-Flame, *back* and *centre*.]

386
Gift of Life

Faring from life to life, you will eventually find LIFE.

« Living means *eventually finding HIM.* »

387
"Score God!"

Over *There* is only "here" in overtime.

[So score God while "*Here*", on home ice.]

388
Your Cure

This here life should be your Cure, not the hereafter.

389
"Where-It's-At"

The earth is man's chosen planet of (Soul-ar) progression.

[If you consider yourself human, then this is *"where it's at"*, and this is where you will have to evolve into GOD-hood.]

390
Good & Co.

Good company, good vibes, good dharma, good progress.

391
« All Demons Are Friends »

To the Aware all demons are friends in disguise.

392
« Great Healer »

Being doubly-blessed with the medicine of my Past and the promised cure which is the Future, the great *Healer* of my life is Now.

393
The Shadowy Three
vs
The Illumined Three

"*Separatism, egoism* and *ignorance* are the three dark triplets of the Great Illusion of Time, *within the small space of me.*"

[Only when these shadowy "three" are banished into the arms of the Great SELF will the sadhaka be ready to reap the Realness of their *Radiant* opposite states — that is... of *Oneness*, of *Compassion*, and of *Knowledge* — shining strong and pure upon the Imminently-Incandescent Face of that Illimitable Space within, which says: "I Am" (GOD).]

394
The Only Sure Sign

To go on and on and on with Sadhana... and never stopping to become discouraged... is the only sure sign that you will get There.

395
"The Sole Cure"

The sole cure to hurtling down in a storm and (subsequently) hurting your wings, is the Soul medicine of looping-the-loop around your planetary blues, as without pause, you drive (& dive) back upwards through the wounded sky, and fiercely pierce on through the burning, azurean desert of the suffering SELF, to GOD's fiery Emptiness of LOVE.

396
Tamasic Tendency

The greatest possible spiritual danger there is to "falling down" is to inculcate in ourself the tamasic tendency to just sit around... and being discouraged... to point our broken, existential finger in self-judgement, self-blame, self-guilt, and self-pity.

397
The Pride of "Self-Pity"

Of all the poor excuses to Spiritually cop-out, the pride of "self-pity" takes the cake.

(It ends up being by far, the darndest of defects, since it is the one recondite pattern which most often slips by unperceived by the frustrated ego.)

[Its formal frown and unfulfilled face, and long sacrificial features fetch forth from the far-flung self upon the Path, a long blue feeling of foiled hope and forbidden fruit, of enfeebling effort and a failed finish.]

398
Ego Will Always Try

Ego will always try to make you give up on your Self.

399
Seek Out the Silence

Seek out the Silence with every ounce of Spiritual strength, for every sadhaka must crash the Noise barrier.

400
Stop!

Just stop complainin', stop wailin', and stop whinin'... and you'll have plenty of energy to go on doing what you have to do... in order to get to where *God Is*.

401
Slow Boat

Bemoaning your sinfulness, your weaknesses, and your errors... is taking the slow boat to Heaven's Gate.

402
Get On!

Forget yourself as a sinner, so what, who isn't?

Forget yourself as having erred... so what, who hasn't?

Forget yourself as being slow... so what, when has speed ever been a requirement of the Path?

Just Get On With It.

403
« Inner Quietness »

Inner Quietness is that quintessential quality conducive to the skillful detection of a lie.

404
Carry On!

How am I ever going to "merit" His Grace?
Why am I not as favored as Sister so and so?
Where am I going wrong in my Sadhana?
When am I going to attain Liberation?
What more can I do to go deeper, faster, and Higher?

[Oh sadhaka, stop Now the how, when, where, why, and what of Sadhana.]

[***"Just Carry On"****... knowing that the Arms of the Lord Encircle you.]*

405
'The Sadhaka of Advanced Sadhana'

The Sadhaka of advanced sadhana must sagaciously saddle the BUDDHA's White Elephant of noble Truth and utter Calm from deep within the Void of his SELF.

[There, he must meet with *maitri*, (a gentle, loving kindness) and with *abhaya mudra*, (the hand of fearlessness), the charging Bull-Elephant of the world's mad, unmindful, desires.]

406
"X" on Happiness

If you wish to put an "x" on Happiness you have merely to desire wrongly.

407
Pure Wastage

To speak without really having something to say truly, is pure wastage of the *gift* and *power* of Speech.

408
"Holes in Your Being"

If you lack in self-control, (and therefore, of Self-mastership), it may be likened to your having holes in your being through which your "Spirit", (or your "vitality"), seeps out indiscriminately.

[Poverty of discipline predisposes the self to an unconscious anarchy of "ego-energy"… and therefore, to a loss, or privation, of Soul-ar power.]

409
God will Care & Carry You

Keep caring for the World and carrying on the Work, and GOD will care and carry you on (through).

410
𝓗𝔬𝔩𝔂𝔰𝔱𝔦𝔠

Silence is Holystic, try it.

411
"Self" Defense

Talking is mostly verbal karate, that is, "self" defense.

412
Incessant Speech

Talk, talk, talk, is the main Spiritual malady of the tongue.
[Incessant speech is the incipient sickness of self-centricity.]

413
Talking for Talking, Speaking for Speaking

Talking for talking takes you away from the God of Tranquillity.
[Speaking for speaking estranges you from the Self of Serenity.]

414
Soul's Strength

The strength of the Soul is Its supreme Silence.

415
Worn and Weary Words'

Let worn and weary words sink into the Silence of the Self, and *be Stilled.*

416
The Constitutional Condition of Consciousness

Stillness-within is the intrinsic constitutional condition of Consciousness... upon which all Real Knowledge rests.

417
Dais of the Sage

Silence is the dais of the Sage.

Serenity is the seat of the Saint.

Peace is the platform of the Pure.

Tranquility is the trestleboard of the Teacher.

418
𝔷erohood Veracity

Next To Nothing There Is Truth.

419
"Sound a Place for Silence!"

Sound a place for Silence and the S<small>ELF</small> will seek you Spontaneously.

420
Glory of Agape

The gate to God glistens with the glory of Agape.

421
Finger of God

The Finger of God Divinely impels every atom to Spiritually impress every cell with the Hum of Heaven.

422
« Body-Bliss »

Body-bliss is bhakti-built.

423
Sacred Drug

God is the sacred drug of the mystics and saints.

[Esoteric Truism: "All who are mystically-intoxicated must be occultly-detoxed in the full Light of Day".]

424
Pyre of Desire

Everyone unRealized, *ignorantly* burns the body alive upon the pyre of desire.

[Spiritual Truism: "Every Love-struck sadhaka *blissfully* burns the body to White Ash upon the pyre of Desire."]

425
Debarkation of Death

Closed is the common man to the Innerly cabled broadcast of the debarkation of Death into the port of his life.

426
Crypt of Dust

The body may be the portal to God; but the body without God is a crypt of dust.

427
Structure of the Universe

The disciplined structure of the universe was built by Divine Intelligence, was architectured by Divine Will, and *Is* maintained by Divine Love.

428
« Clear Cut »

It seems so clear-cut that you cannot "coo", "cuckoo", nor "caw" your way to God.

429
Soul-Languishing Condition

The kama-manasic compulsion for "desire-satisfaction" brings on the Soul-languishing condition of "Spirit dissatisfaction".

430
« A Mind Bending Towards God »

A mind bending towards God makes the passing panorama of the passions weep.

431
"Being There"

Thank yourself, no one else, for your troubles.

[Thank also the Teacher... for *being there* in times of trouble.]

432
"Duty Free"

The doing of all duties detachedly deifies the day, and declares your Spirit to be "Duty-Free".

433
Readiness and Receptivity

The Calling-card of the Guru may be Love, Shanti, or Shaktipat; or it may be a Healing, an Apparition, or a Miracle; but always, It must mold Itself to the shape of the Soul's *readiness* state within, and to the conditional clause of the Heart's *receptivity*.

434
""𝒥all Awake"

As the body falls into sleep at night *you* must fall Awake into the Light.

435
Let Your Gaze...

Look to the Guru's *phantom* feet and let your gaze become Mantra.

436
« Honor These »

Starry form, *Radiant* face, *Smiling* forehead, and *Phantom* feet — honor these in Guru.

437
"Close Chums"

God, Good and Goodwill are close chums; Guru is the fourth Holy buddy.

438
Fruit of God's Sacrifice

The fruit of God's Sacrifice is the man who has matured into Love.

439
Life, Light and Love

Life is the source of Light; Light is the staple of Love.

440
Soul and Mind

From the Soul effuses forth the Sound of Silence; from the mind issues forth the sound of strife.

441
Surat and Shabd

The creative activity of Man's innate Intelligence is made manifest in the revelatory phenomenon of the Surat.

The creative cultivation of Man's core Compassion is spiritually composed through the coveting caress of the Shabd.

442
Attitude of Gratitude

To eat with the right attitude of Gratitude can become a beatitude to the body.

443
Diet on God

If you diet on God then the mind will lead you to the karmically correct, healthful food.

444
"Light" Munching

<u>Physical axiom</u>: "To eat light is to eat right".

[<u>Spiritual Corollary</u>: "To munch on Light is to become Bright".]

445
The Sacrificial Force of All Food

If you are Spiritually and acutely aware of the "Sacrificial force" *of all food* for the sake of the physical form, then the particular choice of food-type (and of diet), is of secondary import.

446
« Stages and Delicacies »

Different stages upon the Way demand different delicacies.

447
"Attitude and Latitude"

A strict eating attitude usually signifies a problem with a certain latitude of mind.

448
Initiation and Nutrition

If Initiation is dependent on nutrition then the Spiritual situation is in dire need of attention.

[You cannot climb your way to God through any palatial preference — in other words, as it has been said by other wise men: "You cannot eat your way to God".]

449
A Passing Phase...

Specific diet discipline and food programming is but a passing phase within a disciple's Spiritual sadhana... but it often seems necessary, and sometimes, even wise.

450
"Smiling Brussel Sprouts"

Students who look like smiling brussel sprouts are not destined to become the Lord's strength.

451
Life Is Life

Life is life and cannot be killed in man, beast or veggy.

452
A Nut's Difference

Dhyanam is not dependent upon a nut's difference.

453
"Light and Right"

If you diet on desire and reduce the calories of need, wish and want, your Being will feel Light and right.

454
Bring to the Table

Bring to the table a benign mind, and the food will be blessed. Bring to the table an angry mind, and the food will be damned.

455
Immune to All Eateries

In the early stages, diet-vibes may influence the mind and meditation, but he who has truly *tasted* God is immune to all eateries.

456
"Grace"

As you sincerely say Grace be humbly aware that God's Grace is descending through you to grace the table and the food with His Blessings.

457
"Love the Food You Eat"

Enthusiastically Love the food you eat... and it will lovingly liberate its essential Energy to you.

458
Heaven Laid-Out

A good table is Heaven laid-out to eat.

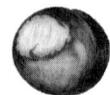

459
The Fuller the Stomach

In the inferior fellow, we unfailingly find that the fuller the stomach, the fuller the mind, the fuller the ego.

460
God's Gullet of Grace

The Spiritual Palate loves to munch on an *Emptiness* of desire, for it is only then, that the whole body-mind comes to Rest... in God's *Gullet of Grace*.

461
The Great Digester, Death

If the ritual of experiential eating becomes too preeminent with you, the *food of days* will tend to become too much of a mouthful to take.

[Therefore, chances are that when the great digester *Death*, calls you to account, your life and Being will remain in the main, still *undigested*.

462
Mindful/Unmindful Mind

The mindful mind has as much power to affect food as food has to affect the unmindful mind.

463
"Divinely-Enriched"

If you are Pure any morsel of food crossing your lips will be Divinely-enriched.

464
"Common Cola and Natural Amrita"

Even as a common cola goes down your gullet, let its natural *amrita* go down too... with the OM'd echo of each God-swallow.

465
« True Prasad »

To feed the hungry is to nourish God's stomach.

[Spiritual Principle: A sharing of the selfless Self *in "food-form"* always invokes the sacrificial Spirit of true PRASAD.]

466
Divine Bounty

Food passed out to a group, that has been Blessed by a Saint's Holy Sight, is indeed Divine bounty for the Spirit's corporeal palm of accrued collective Hunger.

GLOSSARY

Abhaya: Freedom from fear.

Abhaya Mudra: The gesture of fearlessness… usually the raised right palm held outwards in Blessing.

Acharya: Teacher, Instructor.

Adi: Primal Spiritual Power.

Amitabha: the Buddha of Boundless Bright.

Amrita: Divine Ambrosia of the Gods.

Ananda: Bliss.

Arhat: "The Worthy One"; a direct disciple of Buddha; a Fourth Initiate.

Atma (n): The Divine Self; the Soul.

Avatar: A Divine Incarnation.

Bhakti: Devotion.

Bodhi: Illumination; the sacred tree under which the Buddha Awoke.

Brahma: The aspect of Creator in the Hindu Trinity.

Buddhi: The Intuitive faculty of Soul; Pure Reason.

Chitta: The mindstuff; the basic substance of mentality.

Dadi: The always giving, *Father Principle* and the dynamic, gentle *Feminine Force* combined in Name.

Dama: Restraint of the senses.

Darshan: Being in the Presence and receiving the Blessing of a Holy Person.

Devi: Any form of the Mother Goddess.

Dharma: Divine Duty; right action; the Way (of Truth).

Dhyanam: Deep meditation.

Guru (ji): Spiritual Teacher / Preceptor / Instructor/ Guide / Friend.

Haridhana: Treasure of Vishnu; copiously Krishna-like; rich in Christ.
Hridayam: The True Heart; the Heart of Hearts; the Cave of the Heart.

Japa: Repetition of the Lord's name; maintaining Mantra as a state of mind.
Jaya: Conquest; victory; success.
Jnana: Spiritual Knowledge; Divine Wisdom.
Jivatmic: The individualized Soul; the Soul in incarnation.
(Poorna) Jnani: A Sage of Knowledge; a Master of Wisdom; an Enlightened One; a Complete Yogi.

Kama-Manasa: Mentalized desires; the passionate mind; affected astralized thought.
Karma: Destiny which is caused by past actions; law of cause and effect; action and reaction.
Kosa: Sheath, envelope, covering, veil, or body; similar to "rupa" (i.e., having *form*).
Kuthasta: Immutability; Brahman; also, the Third Eye.

Lila, (or Leela): Divine play of the LORD vis-à-vis His Creation.
Loka: A relative plane of Consciousness or Existence.

Maha: Great; (Supremely) Great.
Maitri: Loving kindness.
Manas or Manasic: Of the mind; mental substance.
Mantra: Sacred words, formulae, or seed-sounds which are repeated during meditation; an expression of the "Sound Body" of God.
Moksha: Liberation.
Mudra: A sacred gesture generally made with the hands and/or fingers, having a religious symbolism, or being of mystical import.

OM: The Spiritual Sound of CREATION; the Word (gone forth), the Verb; the Primordial Vibration which sustains all worlds.
OM TAT SAT: "I Am the Truth and the very Beingness of OM"; "I Am That".

Paragate: Beyond the gate to the other shore; that which is beyond and superior.

Paramatman: The Supreme Spirit; the Universal Soul.

Paraparam: Supreme.

Pinda: The extreme, matter-polarized end of the cosmic-physical universe; the most dense plane of existence, that of the physico-material world; the body-mind; the lowest, as well as being the least spiritual of the lokas or divisions of Creation.

Poorna: Complete/Highest/Whole.

Poorna Jnana Yoga: The yoga of complete Knowledge and Divine Wisdom; Self Realization in God through the fusion of the Heart, Mind and Soul.

Prajnana: Knowledge qualified by the Highest Consciousness; Universal Wisdom.

Prasad: A blessed or divine gift; often refers to food that has been offered to GOD, and is thus blessed by Him through the intercession of a Guru, Saint, Priest... or Holy Person.

Purusha: Spirit; the Animating Principle in man; the LORD.

Sadhak(a): Spiritual aspirant/student; a disciple; a chela.

Sadhana: Spiritual discipline and practice; the duties of Discipleship.

Samsaric: The wheel of rebirth; the process of worldly life.

Sant Satguru: A Saint who is also a Teacher of the Truth; not all Saints have a mandate to Teach.

Sarup: A body manifestation, or covering.

Satsang: A meeting of devotees; "the company of Truth".

Shabd: The Divine Sound Current which is said to be sevenfold, sometimes tenfold, in Its keynote expression upon the various (major) planes of Existence.

Shakti: Universal energy of the active Feminine Principle; the Creative Power of the MANIFEST.

Shaktipat: The transmission of Spiritual power (Shakti) from the Guru to the disciple.

Shanti: Peace.

Shiva: Third member of the Hindu Trinity known as the Lord of Destruction; represents the last phase, or the completion of CREATION's Cyclic Process of *generation, regeneration* and *destruction.*

Siddhi: Psychic powers.

Soham: "I Am That"; the natural sound, the subtle vibration, or the Sacred Breath of the SELF.

Srama: Self-initiating, persistent effort in sadhana; steadfast spiritual discipline.

Tapasyas: Purification through sacrifice, penance, and self-discipline.

Vahana: "Vehicle", "channel", or "instrument".

Vidya: Sacred Knowledge; All-Seeing Wisdom.

Vishnu: The central and major deity of the Hindu Trinity, known as the Preserver; Vishnu means "to spread in all directions, to pervade".

Viveka: Discrimination, discernment; right judgement, correct decision.

MEMBER OF THE SCABRINI GROUP
Quebec, Canada
2001